The Omnipotent Sorcerer

The Omnipotent Sorcerer

Roger Aplon

The Omnipotent Sorcerer
Copyright © 2021 Roger Aplon
All Rights Reserved.
Published by Unsolicited Press.
Printed in the United States of America.
First Edition.

No part of this book may be used or reproduced in any manner whatsoever without written permission except in the case of brief quotations embodied in critical articles or reviews. People, places, and notions in these stories are from the author's imagination; any resemblance is purely coincidental.

Attention schools and businesses: for discounted copies on large orders, please contact the publisher directly.

For information contact:
Unsolicited Press
Portland, Oregon
www.unsolicitedpress.com
orders@unsolicitedpress.com
619-354-8005

Cover Design: Kiersten Armstrong, KMW studio
Editor: Robin Ann Lee

ISBN: 978-1-950730-66-7

CONTENTS

Theirs Is A Restless Coupling

Once It Began	12
The Encounter	14
How It Was	15
In Time / Out Of Time	16
In This Dream	17
Allegory	18
Mid-March	19
Pork Tenderloin With Creamy Mustard Sauce & Other Matters	20
Do You Remember Me, She'd Asked	21
Was It A Lie?	22
The Woman With Green Eyes	23
For Debra On Her Birthday	24
There Are Few Risks Greater Than Living A Lie . . .	26

The Omnipotent Sorcerer

After Robert Hughes' American Visions*	28
As If In A Dream	29
Winter Walkabout	30
Crossing The Plaza The Mind Plays Tricks	31
He Came To Us	32
In Their Wake	33
Fathers & Sons	34
The Flimflam Man	35
The Omnipotent Sorcerer	36
On Sunday Hector	37
The First Move Belongs To Her	38
The House Lies Silent	39

The Master Puppeteer	40
Homage to John Chamberlin	41
Free Improvisation After George Lewis's Composition Assemblage	42

To Those Who Cannot

We're Here To Sing	48
A Simple Man	50
A Weathering Wind	51
Improvisation: On The Way To The Airport	52
At MOPA San Diego	53
At The Side Of The Road	54
There's No Substitute	55
They Came To Remember	56
Trust – Or can we?	57
Incidents Of Malfeasance	58
Men With Knives	59
Out Of The Mist	60
They Stand With Me	61
Vet Walks On New Legs	62
On The Brink	63
In A Dark Forest	64
The Woman In Blue	66
Dónde Está **Mi Madre**	67

One Thing Leads To Another

The Street Instructs The Eye	70
In The Field	71
You've Entered Their World	72
Dia De La 'Dance'	73
Marcelo Has Moved	74
It Was May In The Highlands &	75

Maybe Death Is A Gift	76
Q & A @ The Autumnal Equinox	78
It's The Barking Dogs	80
A Lazy Afternoon	82
The Mouth Of The Eye	83
One Thing Leads To Another	84
October 1, 2017	85
Cast-Out . . .	86
See No Evil / Hear No Evil – The Monkeys	88
In Memory Of Compassion, Justice & Honor	89
The Spoiled Child Tinkers With His Toys	90

From: *Sordid Sequences*

When You Remember	94
Un Deux Trois	95
Is That Too Much	96
Restrained Lust	97
When The Gavel	98
She Was The Apple	99
Somewhere	100
It's A Subterranean	101
Some Photographs	102
You May Wonder	103
Especially Present	104
She's Become	105
They Let Him	106
After Broken Teeth	107
On His 60th Birthday	108
Big-Mouth	109
It's Colder Now	110

& So It Begins

& So It Begins 112
& So It Ends 114

For My Granddaughters
Zoe & Noa

With many thanks to the editors & publishers of these magazines where many of the poems in this collection were first placed in print

Free Lunch

San Diego Poetry Annual 2018 & 2020

C A P S Anthology of Poetry 2015

Levitate #2

Chronogram

Synesthesia

Pedestal Review

East Jasmine Review

Jet Fuel Review

Black Renaissance Noir - Fall 2018

CAPS 20th Anniversary Anthology

New Verse News

Theirs Is A Restless Coupling

Once It Began

It was July when they'd met. She wore a black satin bikini & sipped a vodka gimlet poolside. Her eyes were hazel with flecks of gold.

He hung his trench coat over the railing & climbed down to the deck. It was hot & overlooked the Pacific. The gulls were quarreling.

There was a black Lab sleeping next to a woman in a white robe who glanced as he passed. She smiled & exposed a gold tooth.

The bikini shimmered in the sun. The gulls scrambled for the bread tossed by a busboy. He slipped into the water next to her.

The sound of backfire startled the Lab who howled & ran toward the sound. She ordered another gimlet. He ordered a dry sherry. Pedro Domecq.

The woman in white reached between them across the table & left a gardenia with its startling green leaves. Her name is *Fear*.

He had learned to shoot when he was ten & can hit a quarter in the air. She pinned the Gardenia to her black hair & lit a mini Cohiba.

The following day he told her he is called *Sodom* for the darkness & *War* for the hell of it. She shrugged & sipped her cold cocktail.

Amnesia had separated her from history. They spent the weekend searching. She pictured her mother naked stirring a pot of potatoes.

They sleep on a bed with linen sheets. Their fluids have stained the fabric. They read these impressions as stories to be savored.

A man whittles in the olive grove. His name is *Love* or so the joker behind the bar tells them. They buy his wooden horse.

Within a week, they were distracted by letters & phone calls. There was so much to say but without a common language they drifted apart.

The woman in white now wears a red hat & high black boots. She walks her dog behind their rooms. One night she left a sack of stones.

They took separate planes to the north & promised to write. She remembered her first husband had a thick beard & a thin cigar.

On the last train to the city he wrote in his diary: *Black & white needs a touch of red – like a scar across the cheek lights a fading memory.*

The Encounter

The encounter is behind the house. It begins with an embrace & turns to a twisting of truth, fingers clutching skin & bone & a flurry of fists that takes only minutes. When in Timbuktu there's more that worries than relieves. The second meeting gave up a tooth, two ribs & jaundice. The other half of the world spins backward, or so it seems. Soup for breakfast & sour soybeans for lunch. When they meet a third time it's to corral a mutual threat, one who's been plaguing them both with her posse & dogs. They're agreed, it's the menace that's most distasteful & elect to remove her tongue. Jaipur offers those exotic flavors in the mouth that remind the guest of hot black eyes, a wet afternoon & a tender touch. Remember the orchid strewn bed in back of the *cabaret* where she slipped her finger in your ass & manipulated your sweating & your howlin? They met for the last time in the souk where they sell tickets to visit boys or girls & tried to come together. It proved impossible. She'd been *dispatched*, as they say, but it was not enough. Taunts were considered passé so they chose derision. One thing led to another & as night approached they disappeared, one to the east & one to the west. In Cartagena the dark one boarded a ship bound for Marbella while the pale one caught a plane from Buenos Aires to New York. When they meet again, as they surely must, it will begin again. Theirs is a curse. A responsibility. It's been forecast for centuries. Bear in mind, there are many types of torture. Never assume your hands are clean.

How It Was

It was a lie. In a foreign country. By the side of the road. Oleanders. Under cover of darkness.

It was a lie. Rummaging around the hayloft. Through the brambles. That gold coin. Molasses.

It was a lie. & she told it well. Like an artist disguises the truth with her pallet knife. Like snow drifts.

It was a lie. Fumbling under her skirt. Wishing for water. Drilling for oil. Hunting. His last clear shot. Smoke.

It was a lie. Begging to be discovered. Ratcheting up the odds. Sterile music. Open sewers. Sweet cream & Karaoke.

It was a lie. How did we come to this? Why would you say such a thing? What' doess really troubling you? Hopscotch.

It was a lie. Preamble. Sequel. Sequestered. Sold into bondage. Smothered by mother. Love in the time of Jihad. Quarantine.

It was a lie. In your dream of falling. Naked she came & naked she went. All about Eve. All about Jessica. All about . . . Does it matter now?

It was a lie. Daylight's waning. Here's the map. We must go. She smokes a thin Cubana. Blowing smoke-rings, blowing, blowing . . . up & gone.

In Time / Out Of Time

The girl with the white straw hat & no place to hide corrals the man who nibbles her fingers more ardently than her husband does.

When she returns there are three more to share her bed.
One holds a mirror while another smokes & balances on his hands.

It's the girl, the one with the beige dog & green eyes that helps to encourage that first kiss.

**

On holiday in Tunis, Gabriella is bitten by a red snake that leaves her paralyzed & forgetful.

She tries to speak but can't find her way out. That's when the man appears with a map & ten ways to alter her entitlements.

**

When the ship docks earlier than expected, first one, than two by two, the sailors surrender their shoes & promise never to return.

**

In Tangiers, a beggar rifles the pockets of a corpse he's pulled from the surf. He counts the soggy bills & goes to the Mosque to thank Allah.

On Monday he buys a blue suit & an hour with the first woman he's been unafraid to fuck in years.

**

In spring, the houses shake where the rivers merge. It's expected. There's an urgency to open a new road to what may or may not be.

These nights are still without solid evidence of life after death. Walk softly & listen. She could be anywhere.

In This Dream

He's found spinning at the end of an arm of an iron monster bolted to the basement floor. He's a blue specimen from the tribe that wanders the city, without roots, without shame, without duplicity. He's not alone. There's a man in white who runs the machine & a woman in black who oils the cogs. At night when the drapes are drawn back & the moon lights the single window, the room gleams, only the engine's grind & whine can be heard above the moaning in the wings. & Then it's Jim mounting a glossy show of ceramic figurines & flirting with his partner the esteemed Miss Georg who dances naked above the clouds & invites all who pass by. Jim's been dead over a year, but here he is in the passenger seat of a black Dodge Viper chewing a corned beef on rye & sipping a cold Bud. The monster was his idea as was the suggestion of codeine to dull the pain. The adventure begins with his disappearance & ends with his return. There's a debt to pay at every turn. Marsha's portion comes in two parts. In the first her naked skin is stark white with only slight traces of hair. In the second she's tanned a golden brown with perky breasts, a small, high, round ass & Adidas running shoes. Her ticket allows her one chance at the game & only one. In the anteroom, a competitor waits with whittled teeth. Tomorrow the monster will be returned to the museum, the doctor & his associate to the infirmary. The blue man will be placed on the N-Train & whisked to the end of town where the headmaster waits.

There are no second takes – no second acts – no complaint department. It is what it is – Be who you are.

Allegory

After Max Beckmann
1884 – 1950

She'd sailed into this false harbor on the grizzled back of a spotted leopard,
in one hand a burned-out candle, in the other
a glossy bayonet

She pauses at the dock to unpack her catch of eels & monkeys from Madagascar.
Her gnarly crew strips & unmasks, they play catch
with a shrunken skull.

Along the quay, sentinels punctuate the air with a cacophony of unhinged trumpets &
rollicking tambourines - long-beaked falcons hover,
teeth on fire.

In the hotel where gin & whiskey are served, prostitutes lounge on blood-red cushions,
one's chained to a bedpost, another high-kicks & poses
with bullwhip & lit cigar.

She unpacks in the upper rooms too small for the three of them with their lacerated
faces & bearded buns & a shimmy that's ransacked memory & sucked
life's breath away.

One after another the strangers come & go each blinded by dread - with daggers
unsheathed & the song of sorrow on their lips. Theirs is the sodden march
of the terminally doomed.

Mid-March

Dour & lazy from months of stale air & oyster shells, he creeps to the door to sniff the wind for what it may have brought.

In the thicket across the road, he spies a touch of red in the naked vines. Could it be . . . ? No! She would have called or at least . . .

There was a time, not long ago, before the war, before random conflagrations, he'd promised better choices: a ride on the Black Stallion,

the gold ring, Zihuatanejo. She was happy then or so he'd thought, but seasons can be deceptive, you wake one morning in the snow & *Poof,*

a postcard from Barbados, a smiling dark-skinned beauty on the front & the note, replaces her: I love the smoked prawns & Candy's *you-know.*

"Get-over-it." Mother, from her bed in the nursing home, had famously said. & a-s the sun rose higher in the mid-March sky, he dialed the number

in Chicago where she collects her messages: *wear hair-shirts in winter & diamonds in spring – escape waits in the red room along with your galoshes.*

Pork Tenderloin With Creamy Mustard Sauce & Other Matters

Savage. Twist. & Turn. Don't be ashamed. You'll do it. Here. Take it. Ruminate. Rumble-Ramble. On & On. Crank it on. 400 degrees. One thing leads to another & . . . Be careful what you wish for. Remember that time in, where was it, Baton Rouge? The back of Skinny's car? Yeah. You-Got-It. Rusty trumpets. Sour grapes. Hand in hand. & Then. There's that time – You remember – Squirreling away. The ride to town & how it would be. With Him. &. What a time you'll have. & Yeah. You-Got-It. Serious compromise. No. More. Disasters: Tempests & Triumphs. Get over it. Never could get over The Blues. Always bitter. Always bitchy. Always . . . Yes. Oil the pan. Remember. That time. Rub the little fella. Rubb-a-dub-dub. Spice & nice. Chicago. Hot time. That. You-Got-It. Suck. Gently. Of course. & Stroke. Not too hard. The wet places. The dry places. Get drunk & goozy. Yeah. Not her first. Not his either. It's meant to be. &. Why you keep those long legs so close together? Need room to maneuver. You Know. That old trick or treat. You Know. Pop the oven, Honey. Like before. Like that time. Before. The bee-stings. Before. Calamity Jane. It don't need to be like that. It be fine. You'll know it when you taste It. Feel It. Get to It. Let It be. & Here. The play gets hot & heavy. Like Wonderland. Like The movies XXX. Like. No place he'd ever been. & She? She be riding high. Cooing & Clawing. Cussing & Caressing. & Time. Time to stir the pot. Drizzle in the cream. Time for the mustard. Hot . . . No time to waste. Just time to taste. Yeah. The juices. Honey. Down here. Sliver & Slice. Pour on the sauce. Nibble. Nibble. Yeah. Like that. Yeah . . . Just.   Like.   That. ,

Do You Remember Me, She'd Asked

Only your love of horses & the groaning fire pit you insisted we wallow in. What about our swim at midnight, she spat, Joan's phone call, that used condom, the miles of lies you told so well? Need I respond I thought & buttered my toast.

When the phone rang again she'd whispered, you've been summoned, to which I replied, I'll arrive when the rain has ceased, when the hobbled ponies have been sprung & you've been dragged out back in your Dior slip to be stripped & whipped.

She was never predictable. Like the night she rummaged my closet, sliced the sleeves from my leather jacket & stole my prize tie, the one with the impression of Ashley's lips pressed to the cloth. Child's play, she'd howled & laughed her best Hyena laugh.

She thought the same of me. After I'd missed the Rodeo where she'd won the barrel race, where, that night, she'd shacked-up with that fireman from Humboldt & caught the clap – all your fault, she'd said, pissing blood & gasping for a hard-won breath.

That was years ago. That was Galveston & a sore tooth. She's moved to Omaha & raises bees for profit. I call her wise & send presents at Christmas. She sends thank-you notes & last summer a box arrived. She'd stuffed it: bees wax, honey & a cap with a logo: *Bee Pollinating Flower.*

The note: Wherever you stick it, be prepared for the sting.

Was It A Lie?

He would never know & she would never tell

That's how it began. This. Chasing truth. It was Sunday & snowing. The fifth largest accumulation in recorded history – so says Weather Central. She decided to skip lunch. He wouldn't be back until dark. She called for reassurance & sympathy. It was always available. That was the agreement, the pact they had. This other friend – His voice her lifeline. Warm. Gentle. Calming. Maybe. A little corrupt. & Yes. You're right. There was a time when they were *He & She* & so you'll ask, What & Why not now? & she shrugs & says it wasn't the right time & you'll remember her history & how she lied to you too & took that last flight out & appeared again in Miami packing cocaine from Bolivia & Cohiba's from Cuba & a baby & everyone said she deserved better & rounded out her disguise with a scar on her cheek & one over her right breast & claimed amnesty before the next leg that brought her here & now you'll ask to be let out & she'll refuse & turns loose the lemur, her marvelous masked avenger & you'll say, No, not until she tells it all & no excuses & no embellishments & here the curtain descends & the applause begins & she bows to the center boxes & to the orchestra but ignores the balcony & the stragglers too poor to count for much. There are little lies & there are big lies. Tell one & you'll never be trusted not to tell the other or so it is said . . . It's then she's met at the back of the house by the man in black who escorts her to the waiting limousine & you'd think that would be the last of her flimflam & flirtations but to your surprise it seems the baby is yours & . . .

The Woman With Green Eyes

stops to study the pale lavender blossoms of the Rhododendron. He watches from behind his gauzy green curtains as if he were an entomologist & she a curious insect. The weather, warmer than usual, she removes her jacket & unbuttons the top button of her cardigan. He adjusts his tie fearing discovery & backing into his darkened interior, blushes at some singular thought. She climbs the stairs & rests on the tufted chaise. In a moment she will fall into a joyful sleep & call his name. He's in the kitchen slicing salami & toasting rye. The secret he keeps has burned a hole in his head — smoke fills the kitchen. She stretches & her hands flutter. There's a song she sings that speaks of hunger & bleeding horses. It looks like rain. He keeps a Giant Schnauzer in the back of the house & two Siamese cats. She raps gently on the window. He cowers in the corner nibbling his sagging sandwich. Lightening jolts the sky & thunder follows. He hovers under the table, gnaws his numb fingers. There's a crow claiming his space & a buzzard pecking a squirrel's carcass on River Street. The rain is torrential. He whimpers quietly. She raps louder.

For Debra On Her Birthday

August 27, 2019

Out of the mist
        the plaintive call of a wolf
                echoes across the restless lake.

Her plea speaks of solitude.
        Her plea speaks of courage
                Her plea speaks of departure.

Hear me sister, brother, friend,
        I come with peace
               to test our resolve.

Here, one
        avoids anticipation, does not
                distress the jasmine flavored air.

Come, my love / Enter the valley
        free of suspicion –
                free of condemnation -

free of the pain of relentless battle –
        The walk is long.
                The walk is not without quarrel.

Speak of love –
        of temptation –
                of wonder & desire –

Speak of enlightenment –
        Of meditation –
                the senses & the seasons.

The path ascends
    & the path descends
        a shimmering sky on either side.

The wolf's song's
    a distant memory.
        These are the rapturous years.

After Her Zen Poem for Shakuhachi, Viola & Cello

There Are Few Risks Greater Than Living A Lie . . .

Take the time Sheila locked Richard from the house & he burned it down or the last time she wandered away from the fair & was captured by thieves & sold to a hotelier from Marseilles & when the ship foundered Richard answered her call & swam out & carried her back & declared, "All is forgiven." But it wasn't & in the spring when the lights of the town shown green he turned the horses loose & left on his own & the last she knew was a red hot streak in the sky & a note that read, "Thanks for the fire, I needed it in March & the empty bed in May & apples – I've always depended on apples."

The Omnipotent Sorcerer

After Robert Hughes' *American Visions**

The west was snatched up by those who would praise the second coming & they did by ship & horse & wagon & cart to mark themselves successful & they stole & acquired & bought & built & their will defined the time & composition of what was beautiful . . .

I'll have Washington stand here & a flag & a hint of blood & I'll have the Mohicans arrive with platters of venison & bundles of sage & grouse & I'll have a distant valley & waterfalls & a tent & wolves & I'll have a city that cannot stand & pillars of fire & pillars of salt & thick muscled sailors & I'll have guides & scouts & wagon masters, cowboys & savages with black eyes & grease & I'll have a wedding of a blue man & a goat & a woman who'll howl at the edge of the night. I'll have a great war to churn the earth & stir the dead & each race will be ignorant of the other & oblivious . . . & I'll seat my dead hero pensive & alone on his throne of stone & I'll build up & out & higher & higher & flat as the prairie & circular & insular & I'll secure the ridge & fill it with gables & fountains & I'll plant suspicion in the eye of the seeker & they'll be captive to my whim & my fortunes will demand an ear to the east & I'll arrive in my time & in my style be buried by the will of the west & I'll empty my bucket here . . . Here! In the dregs of the past where the present flows & I'll willingly marry & she'll be revered & she'll be exposed & her fact will be flesh & her flesh will be honest & demand your eyes & you may try to evade & turn your back but she'll open herself & insist . . . even . . . now.

* *The Epic History of Art in America*

As If In A Dream

The sweating bull walked slowly toward him head down & lowing. He focused on the horns as bright as chrome, gauged the distance, spurred his big black horse & rode right at him Then, it was then, he jabbed at the swollen head with his pen & missed . . .

His dead parents arrived arm in arm & wanted to join the party & wanted him to kiss them & Arthur, from down the block, came & took off his shirt & displayed his bulging pectorals & offered to box or wrestle or join in a run & he said 'No' because of his leg & when he was sure the bull had come around again he tried to drive his pen between its horns but there was no bull & when he looked again there was only a dusty field & rows of wooden chairs & he took a sip from a bottle & the bottle became a small boy in diapers who cried for his mother & the bull was now a red car racing around the track that surrounded the park where he finally walked without his cane.

Winter Walkabout

It's quiet in the park. Bare oaks, maples & snow. He walks
in frozen air. Minus 10. They'd said, minus 10.
Don't lie in winter. Never lie in winter.

It'd been a torturous morning with her running her mouth hot
as acid. He'd sworn it wasn't his plan or intent,
would never compromise their pledge.

February always demanded more acquiescence than he could promise.
February with its unrelenting weather, its only argument
for sanity, Hendricks on ice & a Guinness back.

He keeps telling himself. Whispering in his good right ear.
More like a seer than a ghost. More like an auditor
of his soul – he never thinks about his *'soul'*.

The facts point to his indiscretion, his preoccupation, his secret. *No
way out & No clear way back.* So he walks & contemplates.
There's always an open bar & he'll find his &

just like that, he skates around the corner & he's descending, not
with a choir of angels, but into the pit that will be his measure
& his newfound home.

Crossing The Plaza The Mind Plays Tricks

There're jugglers roasting a goat & kegs of olive oil, there's
the musk of furtive girls in their summer dresses &
stallions pawing a sandy ring.

The heated air's alive & bristling, fountains undulating red &
green & blue, cops on Kawasaki's & Henry Moore
at gallery La Caxia.

Lovers hover on Miro's silver steps licking flavored ice & fondling anticipation, young
girls dance topless in the moonlight
at Enrique's grill & grotto.

Once a battalion's bivwack, today a cemetery, mottled stones,
alabaster angels, gargoyles & priests in tattered black –
Hoot Owls roost above Gaudi's enchanted park,

paella & pulpo at El Gato Negro, kids in green & white kick a black
& white ball, Carlos ties-off in Parc Ciutadella & dreams
of his lover, Sebastian in Havana.

The bells say nine & corks pop & forks click & somewhere
between Las Ramblas & Calle Laietana an old man weeps
for his disappeared son & somewhere

between Calle Valencia & Calle Grand Via a young woman shivers &
dreams of her lover's brutal cock & braids her auburn hair
over &   over &   over again.

Revisiting Barcelona after seven years – 7/2014

He Came To Us

with blood on his hands, wearing a lion's face & carrying a small boy's corpse in a linen sack.

He came with a lunch of black bread & brie, two clean shirts & a calico cat with one crushed paw.

He'd come to bury the boy & begin again in the south where he'd been told women were chaste & spirits thrived.

He's made a home above the ancient theater. Some say, out back, he's begun a garden of fungi & herbs.

Others claim he's been seen late at night leaving the widow Mary's or the widow Carlotta's or maybe the widow Justine's.

When I see him, as I often do,

he's striding, book in hand, across the plaza or resting on his steps, leisurely plucking a rusty Silvertone guitar.

There are those who speak of the third man, he who can coax the impossible, who dares us to scale the heights, who

will come between us & the river below, between us & the conflagration, between us & interminable fear.

I will not challenge the believers or those who are not. They're entitled, as am I, as is the mystery I celebrate:

as evocative as snow, as instructive as silence, as appealing as a dappled mare running for all she's worth, bent on

triumph & escape, over the hedge, to the place unknown . . . a mere heartbeat away.

In Their Wake

In parts of the Orient bats serve as symbols of good luck, long life, and happiness.

In their wake a fine rain & a common hunger at sundown. All else remains the same: twin retrievers

tethered to a boy's memory of subterfuge & sabotage, a war he could never win, his father, all business &

armed against metaphor, his mother a shadow in the pantry dishing castor oil, wilted spinach & Thursday's liver.

Their wake is calm. He pauses for one last look & a nap at the water's edge. It's impossible

to separate the rising tide from their passing. I walk with it daily as we all must if we've survived.

& the bats? Who will manage their nourishment or corner their fury? They enter their weather at full speed

as if they have no time for council or remorse, as if they've been warned of loss & cautioned

don't look back.

Fathers & Sons

Fathers & Sons. At war. All about town. Under a microscope. Beside themselves. Fencing with the Gods. At the bank. Beside the stream. Swimming with frogs. Annoyed. Anointed. Weaving in unison. Pitching the first pitch. Pinch hitting. His nightmare, Superman, Batman & the Green Hornet. Will it never stop? This volume of mimicry. Buzzards. One for all & all for one. Octopus. Reaching out & reaching in. Where in the world? & how about you? Post a notice. Subscribe & bait your hook. Fathers & Sons & broken wheels & shattered minds. & who remembers the last one? Machine Gun Kelly. Whispering. Without interruption. Spic & Span. It doesn't get much better. Does it matter? Now. Better believe it. & why not? & who's to tell? Mothers & Sons. The wicked witch. Somersault. Who can tell victor from victim? Rationalize. Reverberate. It ain't so remarkable. What about those early years? The record is clear. & clearly green. No doubt. Without a sense of time. Without recrimination. Without so much as a roasted puck. Squirm. Has it always been this way? Never again. Dad. Never again. Mom. Heebie-jeebies. & me without my Coca-Cola. Or. Cocaine. Or. Lemongrass. Or. Sweet Charmaine. Who threw the first punch? Who brought the knife? Remember the dark cloud he carried? Never one for small talk. & me without my ticket to ride. Do you think he ever thought? It never plays out. So much left unsaid. On the table. Under the sofa. On the road to oblivion. Time supposedly heals? Bullshit. Another cloudy day. All that's left. All that's ever left. I guess it's always, laddie be good & all that jazz.

The Flimflam Man

The crafty dodger sets up his card-table at the edge of the park & waits like the Jackal he is – for the sucker in the blue parka with 'Stop Me If You Can' stitched across the back of his jacket & when he arrives fresh from the market or a catch-it-when-you-can crap-game or was it a lazy liaison with his sister's friend Camille, the Jackal strikes. Today it's Three-Card-Monte where the ace-of-hearts slips between two black kings or does it . . . & So - we watch closely as the plump man in the little red ball-cap chatters & cajoles & moves his cards from right to left & left to right until the idea of the Red Ace is merely a momentary memory in the mind's eye & when the sucker picks the wrong card & loses his ten bucks we're not surprised but we are when he asks to try again & again & still again & it's then we listen to the Jackal in the red ball-cap as he chants his chant, ridiculing one disgraced disciple while castigating another & promising great wealth while stuffing his own already fat pockets, promising security & moral certitude while yanking babies from their mother's arms & when the next sucker sidles up real brave & sure-of-himself the fat man in the little red ball-cap claps him on the back & begins his rancid rap again & steals the money again & on & on goes the scam & the captivated crowd roars their unwavering approval & now it seems, even after lie after lie after lie, no one can pull them away from the Flimflam-Man in the little red cap & his mesmerizing Rap & Roll.

The Omnipotent Sorcerer

The bridge crossed in a rush is not the same that spanned the years of his intrusion. Never assumed. Never expected. His act of wicked pleasure should not be rewarded. With each drumbeat, with every ringing of the gong. A hand is raised & smoke, a wand is raised & fire. They're packing pistols in Texas. Next week the funerals. He waves his hand again & blood like rain – cruel weather. Tortured dreams. Dementia & whistling on the wind. He's at it again. See. Humping his way. Fist by claw by dandelion wine. There's much to see from far & beyond. Don't trust his vision. That was many years ago. Instead, walk the master's dog – your way back to the beginning & the building of the way ahead, from couch to saddle to souped-up Chevy to baby clothes to rocking chair. In June they promised documents & an arrested mission. By August hope sprang naked & wet as a newborn. We watched & waited & nothing resembled what had been promised. No matter his vanity, his virulent rutting, his composure under fire, his wrath & ruin. There's not much to believe. Take it from one who knows. Remember how you got into this mess. It wasn't for not trying. Just another dumb turn of the wheel, luck run amuck. By sundown, all will be forgiven. Maybe, by sundown even he will admit malevolence & beg forgiveness. Don't take it for granted. Marshall your minions & prepare for the thunder that is assured. The warning is etched in the stone that bars the door. Read & remember. There are more of you than meets the eye. Trust your instincts. Kiss the one you love & do not look back. There's nothing worth the risk.

On Sunday Hector

left his house early & walked four miles to town, retracing the steps of its original settlers. The path

had seemed deserted with only the cooing of the Mourning Doves & an occasional Cooper's Hawk hovering.

A man dressed in black with a Silver-Fox pelt draped across his shoulders, walked the road ahead.

He steadied himself with a black staff – seven silver bands below its polished silver knob.

That evening Hector & the man shared a meal. The man told of rivers crossed & blood in the streets of the towns below.

Their parting was cordial but quick with no feeling of desertion or treachery. On Monday,

Hector finds a necklace of human teeth on his dresser & a treasure map that promises great wealth to the prospector.

This is not the first time Hector had encountered evidence of trickery & manipulation. As a boy he too played such tricks.

That was then & the tables have turned. He'll leave this house & never return. Before he goes

he'll visit the cemetery where the first of his kind are buried. He'll cut his hand, drip his blood

on each stone & recite the anthem he was taught by his father: *I am Hector a specter among men.*

Those who follow me will be cast out as I am cast out. For us there is no earthly home.

The First Move Belongs To Her

Her mountain bristles in the gloom of another fractious day.
The toads, mute all night, have risen with the rain.

Is this the truth she's come to harness, the lies she's come to burn?
Make no mistake, she's arrived fully engaged & resolute.

In spite of what you may have heard, there are no second takes:
Either in-or-out, your choice. & remember – she's not easy.

It's come to this: Two steps forward, one step back. The night is long.
Entranced, she wrestles with the mist, opens her mouth & drinks.

"Don't fear me," she commands. "Don't tremble in your boots."
"I've returned in the nick-of-time – be prepared for what comes next."

& with that, the set goes dark. There's the steady rain & the moaning
in the eaves. Comfort the lovers in their bed of weeds, the pallbearers &

assassins in their heart-of-hearts incubator. When the gong is struck,
time enough for contemplation & that old familiar raz-ma-taz.

The House Lies Silent

In the distance, an occasional whistle echoes from a passing train. There's a lone firefly flitting among the morning glories & a lone man with a thin cigar wandering in the yard. Now & then you might imagine a woman too, one with long delicate fingers & a wan smile who walks with the man & maybe holds his arm. There's no telling what they might say to one another. No. That's their secret & who would want to intrude – a rejected lover? His or hers – one with a grudge who can't abide happiness, one who thinks spite rules our lives? & as the man makes his way to the gate & out to the tree lined street you might think he feels loss & regret & as he makes his way to the corner & into town where a trio is playing something like *Autumn Leaves* or *Moonlight in Vermont*, you might think he's come to this place to reflect, a place that tells him time is no longer running far behind, but is already alongside & he must keep up or, for the last time, lose his way.

The Master Puppeteer

Clambers up the scaffolding erected for his passage & pleasure. His craft & foolery can't be shared, bartered or gifted. Once, after exploiting the unsuspecting in Phoenix & by way of explaining his incendiary powers, he left a note claiming inheritance from a crazed demonic god – after which, not one has dared to question, cajole or ever threaten. You know him for what he's left behind: a knocked-up daughter, two x-wives & a furious son who's sworn mayhem, vengeance &/or (*Yes*) murder. So we ask, 'What is it that has driven such a creature? What is left to discover & explain?' To learn we turn back the comforter & inspect the sheets: see the stain blood makes when left to harden against the cold, see the stains tears make where they pool under a beaten pillow, see the quivering air that fills the room & rises & falls in blue & purple arcs after years of rage & tumult & fear – see him, his fractured image peering from his dresser mirror, dangling Esther, his puppet of choice, by her nylon strings that he wiggles & jiggles to make her jerk at the end of the rope he's pulled tight around her linen neck. Is this the rehearsal for a forthcoming drama or is it the fantasy of a master puppeteer who depends on a fearsome presence to one of contemplation & mercy to seduce his audience? Tonight will be the test. As the curtain parts, will we find Esther has been dispatched or saved for another debauched encounter? Your guess is as good as mine. Don't wait. Get your tickets now. He may actually be gone before our next sun rises.

Homage to John Chamberlin

There are scraps to consign & configure. Fragments of evolution that have been distilled & disgorged – The guts & skin of the germane & the obscure, the spit & din of a landscape disowned.

Muscles flex. Flames erupt from the belly, dazzling whorls of light & color stream across the horizon . . . Somewhere, among the liberated, there's a decapitated Tucker dressed in flabby armor, emblazoned with the number 6, an eviscerated Checker disguised as a blustery Mustang.

What was once a predictable steel slab has been tortured & tormented – Coaxed into submission – Reborn as water falling or bird in flight or Marilyn Monroe.

Listen: the planet gyrates & elements collide, the grinding begins, the master turns the wheel, eruptions accelerate, levers are pulled, elements are folded & fused & tipped & turned & fractured & bent & from the floor it rises like sabotage or surveillance or bounty or the peculiar marriage of sky to mountain to sea & serpent . . .

No end to possibilities or purpose – To relevance – To integration . . . There may be nothing to eat here – No. There are only those protracted moments to deliberate & meditate & . . . & Yes – Time's up.

Let your levitation begin.

Free Improvisation After George Lewis's Composition Assemblage

In Four Parts

I
Mnemosis

Hear it? The fluttering? Bing. Bing. The squeaky wheel turns & the bell & there's an urgency & calm & flared nostrils & another door opens & another & the ringer is stuck & the buffoon bubbles & squeaks & pop-goes-the-weasel & up pops the conductor with his sliding scale & the chorus with it's will-o'-the-wisp & the cantankerous janitor & sharps & flats & a smokescreen & bellicose babbling & there's that urgency again & now there's running in the streets & a gaggle of wrens & the crime of it all & no one to stop – no one to confess & it's coming closer & it's whispering in his ear & there's the abyss & no one to pull the plug & a cannonade & a colossal wind & winding down & winy-the-poo & the chorus again & its moving away & calling for help & no one's paying attention & *Please!* pleads the woman in red & *Please!* pleads the man in white & what are they up to? Here? In this dark room with the squeaky hinges & the rattling gong? Hurry up. Time's running out. Don't forget the *choo-choo-choo* & there's no one to open or close & no one to write down what's been said. & Who's that? Whistling in the dark? A lullaby? A psalm? Sit down. Let yourself go. That's right. Like That. Just-like-that. Hum along. Honk & Whistle. Hum & Go & Going-Going-Gong. & Gong. & Gong. & Gong

2

Hexis

       Hurry. She's getting away. They're here. Listen. At the center. Whispering. They speak in tongues. Moving out. Arranging thoughts. Contemplating. Step by step. An easy sweep. Wait! They're disguised. Each note brings us closer. Wait. They're dancing to a different drummer or is it a flute or flutterer. & here the dancers turn & no one's left to manage — no one to conduct. It's time to divide the winners & here's where the fun begins. Someone's honking outside. Time to go or . . .? Wait. There they go again. B-Bop & hip-hop & Crazy Eights & why is she crying? Under the lamppost? In the rain? There's a car & a flashlight. A dog or two & a hunter in Black. Bleating. On the wind. That tender touch. He's famous for. That wanton willingness to surprise. & so he does. With Both Hands. & then it stops! No more of that. A race to the center & around the room & down the steps & up the escalator & over the hill to grandma's house & the man in the mask is on all fours & he's not alone. There are three of them & the bus stops here & who will you tell? & Who can you trust? & Wait. It's tomorrow & the sun's right on time & one by one they come from the back into the light & she's in the lead. & Oh. It's been too long. Much. Too long. One by One. They come. In time to the fluttering flute & the whistling orangutan & one by one they slide down the chute & all is forgotten & all is forgiven . . . Halleluiah

3

The Mangle Of Practice

      Maybe twilight. Maybe. Inner sanctum. Maybe. Sleight of hand. There's only escape & a crowded train. It's still raining. Open your eyes & Listen: There are Cardinals & a singing Chauffer. Tumbleweed & a broken hinge. Go slow. This is. *Not*. A race. One. Two. Three. *Twinkle-Twinkle little star*. Run along now. It's his turn. Run. Ahead. Stop! In your tracks. It's a splendid time to meditate. She's crying in the corner & . . . & He's waiting for her . . . Stop. One thing leads to another & Voila! *Voila*, I say. It's incessant. It's a new flavor. He knows. He knows how. Listen: He's approaching from the west. Unarmed. Respectful. & Now. After a little more. Tinkering. *Rub-a-dub-tub*. Twinkle-Twinkle & terminal tremor & . . . Remember to write. & Wait. She's walking away. Toward the exit & . . . & He's running alongside. Anger unleashed. Compromise. Quibble or not. If only . . . He's tempted & she's tempestuous. Come. Take my hand. She seems regretful. Or. Confused. Or. Camouflaged. He winks. His fingers dancing. Hand in hand. Over the river & . . . & so it goes. One by one & two by two. It's an argument. No. A challenge. No. A plea. No – In praise of. A platform. For old business. A gateway. Through which to walk. Butterflies. Rambling Romeos. The donut hole. Escape. At all costs. It's grown quiet. The moon's in a box. Take my hand. Whittle it down. Puff on a fresh Cuban Cohiba. Vanity. Weathervane. In-vain. Whether or not. Hurry. We're almost there. One more yank on the wire & Shush. Baby knows. Tick-tock / tick-tock. Spinning. On the axel. On the end. Of the wheel. Star-light-Star-bright. Spinning . . . Yes. & Yes & Yes & . . . So it goes.

4

Assemblage

      Whatever you find. Bring it here. Yes, the bell too. & the Gong. Tickle those keys. Yes. Up the river & Down the charcoal road. Whatever you find is yours. Is ours. For all who pass by. Rumble. Rugged. Rabble & a Risqué Rut . . . Night falls. Hear it? Like a bucket over your head. Right-on. Smell the earth. Raw & Ripe. Careful. All is not as it seems. Cut loose. Untether yourself. You're not a dummy. She's not a ventriloquist. Lullaby of Bird . . . Bye-Bye. Oh my, how sexy. You sing good. Mama. Kichy-kitchy-Coo It rises in the night sky. A rush to rip apart – to put together. Once. He. Had. A. Once upon a time – He had. . . .Yes. The moaning is in your head. Mumble-Mumble. No time to stand still. Gonna catch a falling star. Bar the door. Without hope. On stage. Swimming. Push back. Don't let it get away. So what if he does shrug his shoulders? Quick. Before it's too late. Gimme the keys. A Blanket of Blood. Like a whispering brook. Like dumbbells for Christmas. Onion soup. Creamed asparagus. What's it to you? He's so gentle. Yes. Like I told you. Can we watch? No time for blowing balloons. Not now. Watch for the Whirling Dervish. Intervals of calm. Never count your chickens. Mercy. Mercy. Mercy. & So it goes. Up a paddle without a river. Hear the hogs honking? Now you know you're close to home. Close to the end of time. Or is it The Dime? They're flying south for the winter. In all their glory. Why worry me now? His delicate touch. Again? No one will stop for his chattering soliloquy. No one? Come on. You have more to say. When the time is right. I'm not afraid. Standing on ceremony. What a gathering. Come on baby. What a mess you've made.

To Those Who Cannot

We're Here To Sing

*"The Dove has torn her wing
So no more songs of love,*

*We are not here to sing
We're here to kill the dove."*

After Judy Collins singing "La Columbre"

Charley got it first. He 'as walkin' out to take a piss an' some sand-nigger son-of-a-bitch shot him in the head. Yeah, right through the eye an' out the back. Jus' walkin' out to take a piss.

I often wonder how I'll get it. Comin' right at my face or in the back the way James got his.

Why you talkin' this way Arno? You gotta believe the sarge. He been sayin' we're covered an' this'll be over in a day or two. All this hostile shit. All this hate for us.

Yeah. All this hate . . .

1
Before the sun's light, I open
my hands on your firm back
the way you say you like it &
run them down your body
the way you say you like it &
move to shape our morning
the way you say you like it . . .

2
The culverts crossed in the rain are stuffed with slaughter and in the desert his bones bake and hers and by the light of a candle a letter is being written and in the supreme city the commander-in-chief warns the world to expect more to die for his purpose.

3
On a clear day in September, I remember it was September 'cause all the kids was marchin' back to school, an I felt proud to be carrying a gun in their behalf an' when I got where I was goin' an' saw the kids we'd killed an' maimed I didn't know anymore . . .

4
She's seen him go off many times and this is no different but there's dread every time. So she puts on her best face and hugging his son to her breast she smiles up at the grungy window of the Amtrak Starlight and waves and holds little Jonathan's hand to wave too and, as if this is the last time she will see him, she makes the sign of the cross on herself and on the baby and in the air and lets that be enough . . . After all, what is left?

5
"The latest news indicates more resistance in the countryside. It may be years before all the subjects are subdued. There will be arrests and many more deaths. We will prevail."

6
In this dim morning light, when the swallows outside our windows wing & whine & pierce the air with their hunt & cry, you offer up

your alluring pitch & peak. The song you sing is for us & we play it together & relish the urge to go on . . . beyond grief

to find light between the dark.

A Simple Man

He has spent much of his life in quarantine, as have his wife & four kids. He stomps the foul field on his way to rescue hope from despair. He carries a load of lettuce, nuts & corn to barter in the camps, has been diagnosed with an enlarged heart & a hint of cancer of the soul. He remembers when it was safe to criticize or join contrarians. He resembles an immigrant from Turkey but it could be Jamaica or even Brazil. He can't remember when being black or brown was not a threat or a curse. He's anxious to revenge the death of kids who died of fever & in chains, speaks Farcie, Croatian, Czech, French, Hindi, Turkish & sometimes Urdu. He wrestles with his need to honor peace & destroy the flagrantly fascist state, grows larger in the waning light, is joined by the passionate & the dedicated. He, as is allowed, turns up the volume & demands the unholy alliance between lies & the law must cease, that honest men & women must seize the day, return righteousness & substance to the ravaged seat of power

A Weathering Wind

You'll notice your parched mouth when you wake, the howl of a dog lost in the vines & streets awash in bristles &

bats & blue frogs & there's your neighbor & her broken son who crawls from the nasturtiums & sings the last chorus. & Vinnie with his

false falsetto who leans hard into the buckling fence & can't remember the odds on number seven (his father's favorite) but can tell the time

Hard Rudder Right stormed away from Rebel Dancer & paid sixty to one & broke the bank on Seventy-Second Street & the time

Jessie broke her leg running from the stranger in white who carried her back to her mother mute & missing an ear & Yes, all this

while the wind empties the fountains & chases old women from church & rattles the door to the convent where Sister Margret meditates & brushes

the long black hair of another lost daughter-of-the-night who's been bought for a nickel-bag & sold for a short pipe & now the wind has ceased whining

& one by one they come from cellars & trash bins & wrecked Chevrolets & from Café Interlude, where we've gone to pay tribute to those who cannot &

when it's time we saddle the mare to the sleigh & disappear down the road with only one place in mind & no one left to remind or remember.

Improvisation: On The Way To The Airport

He'd expected the worst & when it came he reluctantly accepted: Miles unraveling, a bottle or two of the same, a kiss on the cheek from the one who is no longer, the drowned dwarf, skirmishes with machetes, a broken promise, tangerines, milk carton with living spider, mercury poisoning, Saskatchewan. His mother's cultured pearls, blood oranges, his blue suit, her feather boa, a knocking in the attic, swine flu. Mary's orangutan, caramel, the last time she saw Paris, dead deer in the road, the road to hell, Santa Claus, Bambi, butterscotch, hyenas. Florida, Dutch gin, gin & bitters, Bombay gin, gin rummy, gin & tonic. Arthur's curse, her collapsed lung, dishwater, taxi ride, zoom/zoom, misanthrope, miser, mayhem. Dad's gold shoes, Barney's Beanery, Botox & bowling balls, the letter from hell, dissolution, damnation, the road less traveled, her suicide.

At MOPA San Diego

"Open That Door & There'll Be No Turning Back"

1
These boys play at war in a bombed out car, drive into the tunnel of bodies firing through blue plastic blinds.

One has a rubber club he wields like a torch & lights the walls where arms & legs are drained & spread & lashed.

They pass a woman too weak to rise who shoves out her empty bowl – dogs on short chains tear at your legs – each frame's focused on a body

that glows black & beige & cannot bleed / Late in the afternoon mothers come to fetch water & peel back what's left.

One sleeps in a bombed-out rut where the sun might come again & might, on a good day, access the last tree standing . . . the last bridge that connects to nothing.

2
In the younger city, a dark woman wanders the streets remembering a man lost & alone. Another sips from a bottle she's hidden in a black plastic bag.

There's a paper elephant propped against a wall wearing a sign that says, 'Ruptured' & a dwarf who sweeps straw & dust from a crouching tiger.

There's a match-girl's matches but no sign of the tired seller. A river stretches under a wall that begins to sway when we lean against the glass.

There's a bottle in a window that supports a wilting rose where a swaybacked horse lifts a hoof & shuts its one good eye.

There's time for a beer & six sailors & this one young girl. Someone has opened the door. No one comes to see it closed.

After: Srebrenica / Nagasaki / Birmingham / New York . . .
From the Photographic Works of Louis Faurer / Yosuke Yamahata.

At The Side Of The Road

he waits with torso naked for the passersby to see &
touch if they dare

this man yoked, with a gnarled hump &
twisted frame

who comes day by day to offer himself
as the least of us

to remind the strong of the lost, the violent of the humble,
the proud of the weak &

though the air is brittle & the ground is wet,
he comes with cup in hand & alone

as are we all
who wait for our bus that will arrive soon &

with it the inescapable & most perfect fact
we are bound to a future we know not

& will only taste once.

There's No Substitute

for the wish to speak as one, with snakes gliding between the date palms that have always been a problem for the nearsighted & the rats from the four corners bearing plague & missing teeth. A rabid dog died here. Yes. On this very spot. He held on until the cops cut him to pieces & another time, I must tell you, when no one came but the street filled with a thousand cheers & blood ran & bones exploded & we'd watch the games kids invented inside the bodies of the corpses & here was the beginning & the end & now we watch TV with its make-believe & struggle to know the difference.

They Came To Remember

It begins with arrogance & thrives on deception.
    It prospers on lies & is buried in blood.
        It is our history: The Way West.

*

In this photo, she's framed the four dark horsemen against a dense white sky.
Mounted & masked against minus 40 degrees, they search

for the route of tribute, the trail to their ancestors, who lay frozen,
where they'd fallen, finally buried (*en-masse*) on the hill above the creek.

No song –
    No names –
        No stone

Across these plains, on the Res, there's suspicion & watering eyes, starvation, addiction
& suicide.

Today, there's a stillness on the plain – these four are alone & their stiffness makes
their horses skittish – ice clings to their lips, they stomp

the frozen turf, kick up the desiccated snow.

        Chief Big Foot Memorial Ride – Centennial of the massacre at Wounded Knee Creek
            Pine Ridge Indian Reservation, South Dakota – December 29, 1890 – 1990
                                    Photo by Ronnie Farley

Trust – Or can we?
After: "Central Park Five" – A Film by Ken Burns

You be the defendant & I'll be the axe. Ours will be the perfect union. An exquisite wedding

for the gloved hands that clutch the quips & pain, for the politicians & their prosecutors. Yes.

Before long, you'll wake in your own vomit & shit & all you'll remember is darkness, sweat & rats scratching.

Like swaddled mummies, you'll have no voice, no eyes & no chance for redemption.

Lost in the cogs of the machine. *Remember.* Twelve years. We be gone. Twelve years . . .

Who can you trust? Not the axe-man. *No.* Not the jury. *No.* Not the disjointed scales of 'justice-run-amuck.' *No.*

Pray for us mother – pray for them too. Pray or us all. The state is on fire & no one will carry water to douse the flames

in those blood-soaked buckets.

Incidents Of Malfeasance

Damage from the cold? No doubt. A chilly hand is a notorious hand

That's the way he talked. Make something big from something small. Exaggeration? Not so much. Him with his green glass eye

could bury an ax in the head of a leaping deer at fifty feet. 'The One Eyed Wonder' he called himself. It was spring did him in.

Surprised him too. The pitter-pat of an April shower punctuates his amble. His face a gleaming rainbow. Asphalt streaming.

Swollen eyes. Unflinching. Unforgiving. *Bless me Father for I have* . . . Eat your hot dog / Swill a Pabst Blue Ribbon.

Coming up fast. The years. *Time's a killer.* Always made him laugh. Tonight. Alone with his random amplifications: Mommy's late

to the rescue. Pigeons plundered on the roof. Hideout. A safety pact. Dance with dangerous dad. A one way street.

Pay the cabbie. Without guilt or remorse. Where's that winter shroud? That. Cloak of steel? Iron boots? Gone. All gone.

Weep for the fallen. Weep & wish him well. It's only the 6th round – time aplenty . . . or so we imagine.

Men With Knives

Men with knives shiver in the shadows. Theirs is the assignment of a lifetime. Watch the needle move higher. On the monitor. Slip a finger under the strap. Sneak a peek. Car careening. Some afternoons are more comfortable with a reason why. Sly & steady wins the cherry. Bury me high on the hill & under a full moon. Soon they'll come to bargain. No one will be surprised. Some day it may prove possible. Waffling has become common practice. Ask & you too may be disemboweled. Follow the leader up the ladder. With one quick thrust they . . . Can you imagine a world without winter? No matter. Without a pot to piss in? Or so it goes. They left him. Full of wonder. Bleeding in the snow. Or was it a turkey sandwich? Out of line. First. There were antelope at first. Never speak unkindly of an assassin. To live or to die. Fine, I'll have a tomcat. That & a walk on the wild side. Enough already. & here's where the weather turns. Into a garage. Red doors & what's more? Famous for guns & Guinness. Slaughter house blues. Retaliation & revenge. He's just a kid. & him too. Something about time, temper & turmoil. All that's left are the flowers of spring: Lilies of the valley, Lilac, Heather, Ranunculus & Bloodroot.

Out Of The Mist

From somewhere under their shroud of stone the tortured & their torturers speak.

It's a conversation modulated by habit, appropriated by design, shredded by fear. No one complains.

There are walls, gossip, empty beer cans & boots. There's titillation, grenades & dried figs.

It being fall, they drift in & out of the mist ruffling each other's weather, murmuring about gods & courage & . . .

These dark days do not pass quickly. There's the occasional *tick-tock*, cracked tree limbs, bones & teeth.

A star, emblazoned on the forehead of the self-righteous, parts its lips as if to speak – stutters & bites.

No time to reminisce. A beefy cop arranges sympathy wreaths in a circle, scatters petals & thorns.

The conversation turns sharply south. There's talk of blood feud & barbarity. Like old times, they pour on the gasoline.

What comes next is not so much mystery as magic: a randy owl plucks out the pain-master's eyes, a rabid squirrel

croaks in the driveway, the nun's chorus sings *Amazing Grace*, their Bishop plays along, his skinny flute

ripe & randy . . . Neither of us have traveled this far before & may never again. The old maxim warns against submission.

Consider the clenched fist. Stand your ground. There's late frost coming down.

They Stand With Me

"... even if I am crushed to powder I will embrace you with the ashes."
Liu Xiaobo
(Last line in a letter to his wife from prison)

A small, wiry kid tosses a bright pink ball against the schoolhouse wall. He's been at it since the sun was high & now, with the clouds coming fast, he throws harder as if it will warm his body against the cold. They know him in the neighborhood. He's the son of a Buddhist Priestess & the peddler of incense & herbs, named Bing after the soldier David, from the western bible. He's the nephew of the writer Liu Xiaobo who has been away & no one will say more ...

I am not disappointed. I am not alone. My wife comes when she can & brings me roasted duck & sticky rice.

I am not sad. I am surrounded by words of reason & the hopeful murmurings of young students & window washers.

My brother has sent me a picture of my nephew Bing, who practices with my father's sword & runs overland to the sea.

My sister sends word of lovers who've named their first-born after me – I am touched but afraid, afraid for them &

the power of those that hover silently like the vulture who waits for blood to run again - in the streets & fields,

in the town of Tongli, in the town of Nanxun, in the city of Beijing where the tongues are tied & books are burned.

While there's still time, I invite you to the tent where the elephants dance &

devoted aerialists fly

to the waiting hands of another, where a clown, who can wrestle a bear & juggle five knives, balances a big

blue ball on the tip of his nose, to be warmed by the crowd's applause & their belief in possibilities – always – possibilities.

No matter the risk, they'll stand with you

as they stand with me.

Liu Xiaobo died in prison July 13, 2017

Vet Walks On New Legs

"Better that happened to me. It could have killed somebody else . . . I was actually in shape at the time, it's pretty much what saved me . . . I have fallen. You get up. If you don't fall you don't learn anything . . ."

Nick Staback
Recovering Amputee US Army

Collapsing sky. A malamute leads the way. A plastic hand to stir the stars. A plastic arm. A plastic leg . . .

The glacier moves closer. Tears freeze on my cheeks. I smother mom's excited laugh, chew slowly.

How to measure the width & depth of the vault. How to calculate oblivion. When to bite the bullet.

Day one is no answer. Day two is no better. By day ten the fox is loose & running. One month & counting . . .

If not me then who? Summer arrives early. I play hoops with the best. One before the other. It's how it's done.

When the call came, when his number was up, when there is no choice, when it matters most . . .

From the desert to the sea, between calls home & dysentery, after a dinner of boiled goat, after silence & a waning moon . . .

Hunted & hunter dodge the same cracks & crevices, the same muddy water, the same missed shots & rage . . .

'Don't worry' came the call from the fans. 'Don't disappoint your cronies or the marchers with signs,' warned the bartender.

Better the runner with carbon fiber tootsies than the joker with the purple nose. Better me than you.

On The Brink

Hands entwined. A Race to the bottom. Seamless. Sinister. Elation's dead. Poised to leap. Anticipate. Dumbfounded. Free Fall. Scatter-shot. Dynamite.

※

There are *free-metals* alive & swimming under the floorboards of Flint, Michigan. Oil Oozing downstream to the Missouri & Mississippi, The Big Sioux & The James & Blackfoot Creek . . . *Buzzards hover.*

Armed militias are poised to occupy our mosques, our synagogues, our libraries, banks, universities & city hall. *They're encamped:* beside the river, under the Sycamores, on Main Street, behind the barn, in the subway, in your garden, @ Mike's Saloon & Debbie's Cupcakes.

In the suspended haze: Nitrous Oxide, Sulfur & Mercury . . . slag, ash, cancer, C O P D & (Yes) Death . . . *We're on the brink.* As are grandkids, Zoe & Noa, the Smith's boys down the block, little Suzie in Cleveland, baby Norman in Wichita & Mother Maria in Seattle . . . *Buzzards hover.*

Enough. To be haunted by the *tick-tick-tick* in the night – the one who insinuates himself in brain & belly: Oligarchs, Liars, Sycophants, Senators, Charlatans, Buffoons. *Call them what you will. Call them what they are:* Toadies to wealth & power.

Crosses are burning again on our front lawns & in our fields. The Swastika has been resurrected. We're told, "These are good people". An old man screams, "My father died on Normandy Beach. I spit on these *good people.*"

The wrecking ball's at work. *The center cannot hold.* Who will salvage our shattered relics? *There's an eerie stillness.* Before the storm? Before the collapse of what's left standing.

November 8, 2017 – One Year & Counting

In A Dark Forest

1

Suspicion insists: Her owls sweep the air to determine if the expected will come — those who wander like shades

seeking a just conclusion, unlike the peasants he's posted as sentries who dabble at battle & bored,

whistle for the dogs of war — lame & docile as the family pet, overfed & fat from pampering, their bloody paws

still sticky to the touch, still sweet on the tongue, still stain the fragile skin of wounded, raped & living dead.

2

Unsatisfied & undeterred, she assaults the frenzy of hail & blistered skin. Not her first engagement

with combat. Not her last. There, where the first blows were struck — see how she straddles the enemy's lines, bites back

the sentence of defeat. It's always one, two, three & go on. Never slaughter your neighbor's best & brightest. Always

plant the unexpected. She can't remember being surprised, remains unwilling to pretend. Winter awaits the sunburned flesh.

Protect what it possible & forget deceit.

3

Alive. Above or underground. Wasting away like wind, the triumphant straggle on, lips curled to grin or sneer,

the first defense of choice. From town to town, where the monkey sleeps, where the hunters extract the seal's strangled song, the otter's bleat, shriek of possum, yowl & yap of cornered coon. A system of comings & goings.

Militias wed to war – Oblivious to the impassioned pleas of the guileless among us. Days: Adrift in the silt of judgment.

Nights: Playground of the disengaged.

The Woman In Blue

played the guitar & offered peace & when she entered their town she played a melody rich with pity & love but tempered with doubt & the men & women & kids & dogs & all that walked & some that hobbled came to see the woman in blue & were offered, each of them, one wish & when the day was done the woman in blue took up her guitar & they sang & danced & one by one they remembered their past & how their wishes were always denied & wished it would not be again as it had been & one by one they promised 'No' & 'Never Again' & the woman in blue played for them & all was as it might have been before & they promised again & assured her again & she left with their promises in her purse & it was some time later, but all too soon, the men & women stood again for the killings & no reason other than what some priest or president had demanded & it was then a blanket of sand came over the town & all its inhabitants & their skin & hair & even their teeth were coated with sand – all but their eyes – their eyes that had once been blue or black or brown or green or gray were turned to chalk & that is all they would ever know & all they would forever see.

Dónde Está Mi Madre

A child weeps & her cries reverberate throughout the dingy warehouses,
makeshift barracks & swarming
extraction camps, it

ricochets across the desolate plains of west Texas & southern California &
southern Arizona & the mesas
of New Mexico.

A child weeps & his tears threaten to drown the tongue-tied Christians, Jews
& Muslims, they dampen dinner tables
in Portland, Maine &

Poughkeepsie, New York & St. Louis, Missouri & across the Rockies &
across the sea to Honolulu. Children weep &
parents weep &

a once-proud people cringes in the wake of what it has allowed & what it
has wrought & what it is to be
dishonored.

Between bouts of fear & trembling these kids are heard to ask ¿ *Dónde está mi madre?*
– ¿*Dónde está mi padre?* –
¿ *Dónde estoy?*

'Where Am I?' rings off-key like a cracked bell – like a symbolic "liberty"
bell, cracked but still resonant, reminiscent
of what has been lost but might still be.

One Thing Leads To Another

The Street Instructs The Eye

Random snippets of debris emerge from the cracks & gutters
of these Paris streets.
The Princess Tree blossoms & dies, marking time & place in passing.
The eye knows & the river
follows. There's the *tick tick tick* of the town clock & a hand to
catch the feathers when
they fall. Here, even the pigeons prance & the dye is cast, here
he's left a blue suitcase, a
banana peel, sparrows that peck at the stars, an apple rotting.
A dead squirrel rides a rush
of water from an open hydrant. The actors are nowhere to be
seen only evidence of their
passing: bricks & steel chains, mortars & a wire fence, balloons
adrift & a flowering pulse
where feet might be – busted boots & tourniquets. After the riots,
a blend of tickertape &
bloody gloves, after nine years, history mocks the rabbit trapped
in the eagle's nest. Beside
the blue suitcase a pistol, a human tooth & a pair of red wool socks.

An Exhibition: Photos by Jean-Luc Moulene - Dia Beacon 12/17/2011

In The Field

Far from the sea, the puckered husks of barnacles ornament the hull of an abandoned skiff.

Through a hole in its dilapidated side the vision of a cross, vague but enticing in its shroud of fog.

The men that hauled this wreck from the sea to find a place on this hill made no mention in their diaries.

*

In town, there's one who remembers but will not tell. We thought, after the death of his only son, he might . . .

The field hasn't been plowed for years. A stump or two attests to history. Tire tracks speak of a rendezvous – bones

scattered in the tall grass, faded photos in a box, an empty whiskey bottle.

*

A raccoon sometimes sleeps in the shaded bow of the skiff. On Sunday, you might hear the chorus from the church below

where parishioners pray for time to settle scores, to emerge arm in arm in the eternal oblivion.

Dark clouds mass on the horizon – a rising wind. Salvation is a matter of caution & good fortune.

*

At midnight, a feral dog howls under the thunder, gnashes his teeth as hail hammers against the closed church door.

Lightening darts across the graveyard, scatters the shadows, frames the weathered markers

where the secrets molder & the sleepers bite & claw & wrestle their reverential demons.

Inspired By A Photograph by Patrick McMahon

You've Entered Their World

by water & wind & to these naked villagers you seem a God. They

toss you bouquets & oranges & you kiss their babies before dawn
finds you clothed

in a sparkling tie & Armani suit squatting in the muck at the edge
of the swamp

where you've come to gnaw the thing in your hand that drips blood
on your chest with every bite.

Is it the lion's heart lost on the long march or is it your own dark heart,
the one with the fragile mouth

that speaks to the dead & wanting, carved from pumice & lost in time?
Is this the end you desire,

scuttling remorse in a pot of pity? Be ashamed. This is the last island
in the chain. Don't lose your compass.

There's much left to reveal . . . Don't be a fool . . . Not this time.

Dia De La 'Dance'

The pillows are full & the dancers are full & the singers roam unscathed & she appears & kicks some ass & the stammering bodies are sucked up a tube & their crumpled skins are left to rot in the rain. Reindeer shuffle & strut, waddle & lurch & he is the explosion & the mask, the incendiary & the flaming wall while she's the queen of drag & that one too & him with his slippery copper skin & they rampage & curse & clamber up on pointed joints & inflexible toes bearing the pain of evidence & the trial of exasperation. One by one they hug & giggle & scramble to the top of the mountain where air is pink with pollen & no one lasts long & the rhythms are deafening as are their pleas for resurrection. Two by two they challenge territory, flinging smoke & starlight across the mumbling fumes & pious cigars, whispering feet tapping code only the blind can read. They unite in a swarm – disciples in their desolate dance . . . to heaven or hell whichever commandeers lethargy & welcomes them first.

Marcelo Has Moved

& he's taken his illustrious, his most willing, his ingenious ingénues in crepe & candy-apple-pink & one by one ensconced them upstairs where a wanderer from Turkey or Tibet may, at any moment, come & nuzzle & fondle & interrupt their sleep & toy with their transgressions & . . . & anyone at any time may come & unwrap the wicked Wanda from her revelry & the pixie Precious from her snicker & snooze & when the time is right you too may want to visit Violet & Virginia & titillate a tight valise or probe a puckered synapse or wrestle with Robert the Robber who lurks along the Wailing Wall & Yes – there's even time for the faint of heart to hearken to the song of the smithy who forges the chains & the executioner who slings the axe & waltz with the widow in the willowy gown who weeps all night & runs with the rude & ruddy runner in purple tights who blows you kisses & will let you nibble her nosh for a petty price or pet her pony for a penny & if you're specifically meticulous & resourceful there will come a time for the goats to bleat & the roosters to lay & it's then you'll gather your wits & a silver goblet for luck & shake his hand & wish him luck & pack a box & mail yourself to Galveston where a tiger waits & a ship to Barbados & Miss Molly Malone.

After: *"Marcelo's Staging & Design"* – Barcelona, Spain

It Was May In The Highlands &

the man who stole eggs from the laboratory drizzled beet juice on his cabbage salad musing on his exploits & the likely harvest in the basement where jar after jar was filled with squirming multitudes soon to be released & the phone reminded him of his romance with puppetry & the conquest he'd dreamt last night & the bus driver who tailed him to the river calling his name & padding around his tent with her malamute named Tarzan & who'd brought down an eight hundred pound Elk single handed, carving his initials under its chin with his teeth, telling the tale on drunken nights to one prospector after another who called his name & urged he repeat for the thousandth time the blood trail to the barn where the hogs divided the carcass. Christmas came early to the encampment. There were bones & an ever-shifting population dependent on mayhem for amusement & gratitude. That was before Saskatchewan Mary arrived with her entourage & stories of the great war without which the chosen *leader-at-all-costs* would have lost his head at the table & the million he'd sewn in his underwear, this being that time-of-all-times when sacred cows were slaughtered for the amusement of the throng & crippled kids who hung around for the cast-offs & free sex with the used, cursed & despoiled. Never let it be said there was never fairness afoot & enough to-go-round.

Maybe Death Is A Gift

We spend our whole life trying to stop death: eating, working, loving, praying . . . All we really know is . . . Nobody comes back.

There comes a point in life, a moment when your mind outlives its desires, its obsessions, when your habits survive your dreams – when your losses . . .

Maybe death is a gift – you wonder.

David Gayle (Kevin Spacey) - <u>The Life Of David Gayle</u>

He's often seen rummaging the detritus in the alleys
behind the small shacks that straddle the floodplain
at the edge of town.   His is a stranded life.

The collection of junk he whittles & glues,
welds & polishes, chisels & hones to sculpted
bounty can't account.   It found him one night.

February. The weather milder than usual.
He'd been drinking at the tavern in town &
walking home – alone – when it jolted him

like a bolt thrown in a once solid door. He's never
been the same. You could say *epiphany*, he might
say *eternity*.   It seemed to stifle him.   A year

went by & another & then, rising up, as if driven
by some primal, subterranean force, his precisely
rendered sculptures began to once again accrue.

His alternative to dread? A tenacious longing for calm?
Is *stranded* too severe? We all hover at the edge
where eternity waits. We're all,

in our own way, *stranded* – dragging one more rock,
up one more mountain – for one more brief
extraordinary view

Death is a gift? You wonder.

Q & A @ The Autumnal Equinox

It's Wednesday & you're planning another rendezvous complete with maple syrup in upstate New York when you become obsessed with a hyena suffering a panic attack or is it a tiger with a toothache? Maybe a memory of a slow dance at the juke joints of your youth, the ganja that kicked your eyeballs back a few notches, the woman who worked you up & down & up again, the bait & switch that got you a broken mouth & a quick trip out of town? Who knows? *The Shadow do*. Sure as hell these random thoughts are a plague to be doused with lye – quick & sure. Obsession is a curse you cradle like a stillborn goat. Time to bury it – once & for all – Sucker. Keep telling yourself. It's bound to work eventually. Do you ever hear from her? She left in a hurry. When was it? A year? No. More like two. Yeah. Two years. Busted you up for sure. Steady. Steady now. No need to get your ass all jumpy. It's only conversation. OK. But. Remember. I'm all you got. Better be nice. Never can tell when you'll need me again. & so it goes. Year after year. You motherfucker. Slam one door & you creep under the next. Badger. Bully. Bastard. Yes / No & Wolverine. Snatch what you will from any who grind by. Destroy the body – No – Eviscerate the soul. Rattle around inside the shell 'til all that's left is the hiss of gas as the corpse cooks. Need we go way back? Strictly relief. Not random ambition. Not clarity. Too late for clarity. Dredge it up. It's your thing. Scatter the leavings & let the buzzards clean the mess. No better guide than a two-bit hustler like you. Careful what you say. Don't be getting ahead of the story. What escalated with her brains blown across the shattered glass actually began years before. A fact. You don't say. You mean the time in Chi when you scammed your way from bar to bar & waitress to waitress? Stealing just to get by? No big thing. A little here – A little there. & then you got clean? Not for long. It left a bad taste. So you went on to crystal. Nice change. Lucrative. Fancy. Feel better now. Asshole. You're ahead of the story. Again. Yeah. It was years later. After a rotten marriage, a deserted kid & first sculpture. The one that sold. It was London at Christmas. Cold, wet & full of attitude.

But. Yeah. Exactly what I needed. & hanging-out on the Costa del Sol, tripping to Morocco to find Paul Bowles in Tangier & San Fran that spring where it began in earnest: Adrienne executed, Ted to Folsom, burned for twenty grand, R leaving for a warmer bed, studio trashed, eleven years of no new work & on & on. & After that. After all that I buried the last of my stash & never looked back. Crazy. Lost your nuts? Turned your back on everyone. Poor baby. Shut the fuck up. I don't answer to you. Never did. Never will. Not much left to salvage. & then the old man dies. Yes. Dad dies & all bets are back on the table. Never knew how freeing that would be. Life begins again. Really begins. Oh? Yeah. There're those who survive & even grow with papa. But? Not the rebels. Like? Yes. Like you. Spoiled. Center of the universe. We're all the *center of the universe*. Ask anyone. I have. &? No comment. Let's move on. Right. On we go. *Beep-Beep*. When was the last time? Last Time? Yeah. Last time you let yourself go? You know. Gone. Out-of-control. Spontaneous. Burning to be. Racing to catch up. Free? Shit. I don't know. Maybe never. Maybe last week. Maybe in Cataluña. Anonymity's a relaxing mask – even your shadow's ignored – there's freedom in that. Being alone has special value. No judgments. No one gives a shit - A blessing in disguise. Except. Except what? No matter where you go, there you are. Ain't it the truth. Life's a bitch. & they see you coming. Always. One beach to the next. Yeah . . . Up the road & down. But - Let's move on. Whatever. I'm bout ready for a change. Why don't you take a hike. I'll take it from here. Not much longer. It'll be winter soon. Solstice. Right. The cold end to a hot hand. See you on the other side. Watch out for bad sushi. Good Luck. Rock & Roll. & . . .

It's The Barking Dogs

I

It's the barking dogs that terrify, or so she says, to one who wouldn't know the difference. It's a gamble either way, says he, who would be next.

Was it ever any different? & if so, who can testify? Who is still alive or even sane? It's about discovery. Has always been. Only zealots,

saints or sycophants bow to such spiritual swill. Wait! Listen to the water-god grumbling in his cave under the sea. One for you & one for me.

Justice. It's what's being preached these days. A kind of mantra for the weak & sheltered, the possum & the snake, the skunk & Polly's boy-bride.

Or is it – boy-groom? Each role unique. Each costume instilled with love & castigation. March on before the curtain falls & the hero is heard to weep.

There's a rendezvous at the mountain's crest. One after another they come for their final accounting. She will determine the order & who will wear

the crown. So little time. So many men – so many women. Time enough when the blood runs cold & I lie down but to sleep in bed . . .

2

Surely you're joking, she rails & out-of-turn at that. Shame on the tamer, that ragged excuse for decorum. Who but you would disarm the issue?

I speak for the desperate too, he mocks, those who cannot get out-of-their-own -way. & what of those who come at night warbling for peaceful sleep?

& what's become of fealty in this time of frailty? Where's the spine that binds, the glue that once meant cohesion – not the dearth of trust? Hogwash,

they chant from the balconies. Give us our daily dose, our diet of rants & red-meat, platitudes, pick-me-ups & promises galore. Why waste

another day without the reassuring aroma of horseshit & the pontiff's dirty laundry? At which point, she wails, there's more to gardening than

digging in the muck. & what of chastity in this time of lust & lascivious meandering? To which he chuckles, chastity be damned & hypocrisy with it.

Whoever said it would be easy, this business of balance, of defying equivocation, of weathering years of bulls-run-wild, of rampant blasphemy?

The crafty magician moves the little ball from shell to shell to tease & tantalize those who would even die for one more chance to be duped.

A Lazy Afternoon

Parry & thrust, thrust & parry. Round & Round they go & where they stop – up pops the weasel & why not? Surely you do not tend to offend or is that too much to expect & expect she did & now was her finest hour or so the good book says. One wrong note & *Pop* goes the coo-coo & who's to tell & who's to care & where in hell are my riding boots, asks him, scrambling to be first in line for the long ride south. Who indeed? As for the rest, they take it on the chinny-chin-chin & rummage among the bones & roses for that last glimpse of him & her together for their afternoon delight or was it cribbage with cocaine & wine & the luxury of a pool table in the dining-room, fellatio, cunnilingus, a digitally stimulated anus & a Harley on the porch – wouldn't you know something would come up & bite him on the cheek & so it goes from one disappointment to the next with giggles galore gone with the wind & no escape for the forlorn or fermented or was it fornicated? Not in the face of vanity & mommy dearest racing the last race with gritted teeth & sour breath & the gang's all here & Ruby to boot with her sterling silver buttons & bows & that old Martin she treasured since the beginning & here she comes again, wearing down resistance & strumming for all she's worth, which is a handful & no one the wiser & here's where the script changes & a new set of players enter stage left & we see, for the first time, Richard without his customary entourage wearing jockey briefs & twirling a brass baton & the entire cast sings in unison *Hallelujah, he's a bum* & off they go & here we are again unraveling our map & teasing out the last bit of memory for the last ride on the last horse in the last race to the last encounter down the last hole to the end that is inevitable – & so it goes.

The Mouth Of The Eye

Famine drives the mouth to eat the raw and charred alike. No country has been crossed that does not attest to this.

Certainly not here, at the marriage of Frankie & Johnny, the place where truth & lies thrash-it-out to the last breath.

Not here, where rivalry is sacred & the first one through the door with sustenance carries the banner & the key.

She's been working her way across the plains, into the mountains & down to the sea — nothing has changed her, nothing has

replaced the void left by months of bloodstained sheets, mother's drunken rants & Brandon's cold corpse.

The mouth of the eye knows what it takes to assuage hunger, what must be said to call off the dogs — hyenas in the underbrush.

The mouth prepares for his arrival — he who would carry her away — to an altered view — where green is not only the color

of pummeled flesh, where a quick boat does not only imply escape, sunset a reason to bolt all doors. There's still time, the sea

is warm & welcoming, let it open & caress you — savor the scent of plumeria & kukui, the taste of cinnamon & clover.

Whatever summons, whatever follows, stifle your fears, your cries for revenge & toast the time that patiently waits — the end to shame.

One Thing Leads To Another

Up Camden Road to the top where your pierced ear is at home with the punctured tongues, tattooed backs, spiked hair, spiked boots & rummy eyes the size of hubcaps – to Royal College Street & a feta omelet flat & soggy & The Congo with its deposed & scarred & Asia with small tight breasts & hot chilies & through the maze of The Barbican & Tony Oursler's talking clouds & lunch with succulent mussels in garlic cream & James Joyce alone in a box & the tears of Paul Gallico at Dunkirk & my Grandfather Ben & his brothers on a ship from Odessa to a new life until, deep in debt, he parked his cart of scraps & junk, walked back to his dogs & succumbed to poverty. My father insisted respect be given but called him "foolish" behind his back. It was a time when Ragtime played & fathers hid in basements & toolsheds, left on barges, hitched-hiked to the west & salvaged what they could from bins & baskets & roadside dumps & in the hobo camps of Illinois or Missouri or Colorado they told of fine horses they'd ridden & women they'd loved & in the daylight they'd hide their sweaty clothes & gawk at the bejeweled wives of other immigrants far more brazen & luckier than themselves.

London 2011

October 1, 2017

Tick-tock. Fire-in-the-hole. *Pop-Pop.* Honky-Tonk. Dancers enflamed. *Pop-Pop-Pop.* What was he singing? Did you hear that? From Sun City to Sin City. From meticulous to chaos. Atop the heap. Dissection & Dispersal. *Pop-Pop. Pop-Pop.* Runaway train. Fissure. Tell me why. Fracture. He covered her body. Without mercy. Massive explosion. A nice guy. High Roller. High flyer. Heaven sent? Whose to say? 500 rounds per minute. Bee-sting. Blood-Oath. Bound to die. The band played on. & then All-Hell. & Oh. Hell. Mom & Dad. Baby too. Run. *Run.* Run. In extreme circumstances – *Pop-Pop Pop-Pop.* 22000. Hard to miss. Fish-in-the-barrel / bodies-in-bedlam. Lay my body down. We're here to sing. Bullets & eer. Barely alive. Sirens in the night. Not quite Gomorrah. Not quite god's house. Up Up & away. From the 32nd floor to the River Styx. "Save my baby boy." What a man will do. Can do. Has done. The air is forever haunted. His room is now closed. Where there was wailing in the night. Silence . . . 57 dead. Over 500 wounded.

Viet Nam? No

        Syria? No

                Iraq? No

                        Las Vegas, USA . . .

Cast-Out . . .

Cast-out. Castaway. Casual. Cunning. Cruel. Corrupt. Candid. Condensed. Condescend. Cornered. Covered. Corny. Clever.

On the other hand. From her backhand you'd think . . . Stranded. Startled. Studied. Staunch. Stern. Strangled. Struggle.

From time to time. That was quite a feat, he said. Whether or not. Without a second thought. Temporary. Tumescent. Triangular. Tonight.

On the march south . . . Originally there were six but now . . . Miles to go. Munitions to buy. Morning-glory. Monsters to slew. Mothers to love.

She came with arms outstretched & her hands . . . Overcome. Ocelot. Ostrich. Octagonal. Outboard. Overkill. Out of the dark.

Mark you this . . . Somewhere in back. Summersault. Salute. Sauté. Singular. Suspicion. Sonogram. Surreptitious.

From the basement . . . No one was left. After all these years. Nonsense. Nuance. Nincompoop. Niacin. Never again.

From what he'd read . . . Over the transom. Out of the box. Under the bed. Behind the barn. Between the sheets. A shovel of stars.

The one who initiates . . . Bubble-Gum. Broken Arrow. Eros. Hercules. Stagnation. Worrisome. Weather Man. Wonder Woman.

If only she'd told him. What was her name? Who holds the cards? Quicksand. Sodomy. Singular. Hot-To-Trot. Enigma.

Name the final four Ports-Of-Call. Unwrap the sausage. Heat the pan. Buttercup. Braggadocio. Berlin. Vanilla. Vacuum. Mumbly-Peg.

If truth be known. Airtight. Aroma. Arsenic. Armageddon. You're under arrest, she said. Fuck-You, he said. Mass Incarceration.

Moonscape. Monster movie. Minuscule. If & when . . . Helter-Skelter. Shoebox. Submarine. Open for me. However you want it.

Slumber Party. Sour Mash. Succumb. Birthday Cake. Binary. Blitz. Orangutan. Oscar Wilde. Window Washer. Effortless.

Here comes the bride. Eruption. White & Withered. Worried & Weathered. It's you last chance. Tell it to the Judge. Crackerjack.

Beyond-The-Pale. Out for a run. Unperturbed. Neglect. Nowhere to hide. Sunday. Soothing. Random. Toothache. Act of kindness.

Just suppose she . . . It's never that easy. Bottlebrush. Booby-trap. Bongos. Smorgasbord. Silhouette. Cantankerous. Sunlight & Sabotage.

She never came home. Over the hill . . . He wouldn't take her back. It's been a long time between sex & sanity. Mercy - Mercy - Mercy

New Year's Day 2018

See No Evil / Hear No Evil – The Monkeys

History speaks of betrayal by the father of the son – the mother of the daughter, speaks further of betrayal by men of women – women of men – by leaders of the led, in fact, we often betray ourselves

**

What of the menacing wolverine

loose in Siberian tundra? Villainess
Marauder, say some. Defender
of integrity, say others.
That bitter curse, like a kick
in the groin, blurs our appetite.

We're surrounded by whispers meant to disarm,

to distort the muddy soup we call 'vision'
while obliterating bravery or better – guts.
How to slaughter the rabid wolverine? How
to marry hope to confrontation, how to salvage
truth from this naked & corrupt comedy?

What's become of comity?

Like a bittersweet cup of hemlock-laced
Cabernet or arsenic baked into a plump cherry
tart, temptation is deliciously & deceptively
life-threatening. The table's set, wine is poured,
who will dare to lift the cup of defiance?

September 2018
Remembering Senator John McCain

In Memory Of Compassion, Justice & Honor
For Senator Susan Collins

I am your devastating, willful & intoxicating nightmare. I am the conscious you have displaced, the spy in your house of hypocrisy.

When you brush your teeth & glance in the mirror, you'll see me over your shoulder, when you take your morning shower, I'll be holding your towel.

When you mocked '*Advice & Consent*' by ignoring facts in favor of personal political gain, you opened a door too often locked & invited me in.

& Even though I may be easy to denigrate or deride, I'll still be at work inserting myself deeper in your psyche – erecting headstones etched with the names

names of those whose lives will be abused, displaced or even lost by decisions made in your name, your history, your discharge of '*duty.*'

Oh – I know you're not alone in this. Your compatriots share the blame – yours however is distinct – you were the critical linchpin & as such

bear the curse alone – the weight of which I will wield over you all the days & nights you have left on your way to your grave.

October 7th 2018
The day after Judge Kavanagh was confirmed by the US Senate

The Spoiled Child Tinkers With His Toys
(To Be Read Aloud With Increasing Emphasis On Tone & Volume)

Out of the fog – out of the grunge & fabrications of truth - stumbling one pathetic step by corrupted step – our little *bebe* – our child from hell rampages blindly,

gutting our neighbor's trust - bent on deceit, sets flares & fires in their backrooms, seduces the naive & jaded alike. No one's left to trust. No one's left unscathed.

He levels his malevolent gaze at the weak & small – children are his favored feast, their incarceration his preferred scheme – The rest of the planet be damned.

As he waddles to his next encounter, his tricycle becomes an atomic scooter – the next big-bang will be his rollicking mission to corrupt . . . Fists will fly

in the walled city he calls his colony of ghosts, where Hitler holds court & he, the little one, sits to the master's right – his tiny gloved fist clenched in salute.

Our bitty *bebe* pouts when the spotlight fails to illuminate his pronouncements – screams for his fanatic toadies – rants & roils when disobeyed.

He demands the rule-of-law be abolished. He is the law. He & only he can carry the plan afoot – the one where he reigns eternal – the one where

only White men & White women attain absolute franchise in matters judicial &/or sacred. One for all & all for the blessed apostrophe in charge.

& that *apostrophe* diddles all night – rises before dawn to spew his syllabic rancor like poison over dining tables, boardrooms & desks of the enlightened & naive alike,

those who have relinquished all responsibility for what is being said & done in their names – what this aberration concocts & decimates is OK - or is it?

What say you? You – who are being driven out of your 'united' states-of-honor by this rabid-dog-of-a-child gone berserk with power – this narcissistic clown bent on destroying all the trappings of personal sovereignty, righteousness & sanctity we as a nation have won these 243 years?

Not one covenant seems out of bounds – not one hard-won freedom is to be protected. We are in the hands of a clueless, tyrannical child & It's time to put him down.

From: Sordid Sequences

When You Remember

When you remember her glazed eyes, blood pooling under her head, gun in her lap, *Pretend* whispers in your ear, a favorite prayer she's adopted for these occasions: "Forgive our transgressions." *But Mom*, her sweet essence spouting caution & irreverent platitudes, like, "Get over it." & "She was an adult." As if the winds of time whistled through her head & billowing sails drove her forward, where steering is a chore & sleep the only passage. No more of that. The dais turns & the speaker unravels before your eyes. Who's left to corral the victim? It's here we've gathered to separate guilt from truth, to render what's left & claim the day. Whatcha gonna bet there's not much left to decipher let alone divide. Praise is no lunch, merely a vacant morality play. Cash in before the lights go out.

Un Deux Trois

un deux trois / un deux trois. Let the play begin. & with that, the drummer. Pretends. It's around midnight on the Sahara, you're alone, there's a sandstorm in the distance that blocks the moon & over the dunes comes Michelle with that quirky smile, a cold bottle of Veuve Clicquot & her purse filled with those cracked & broken promises. To say, "No" would be impolite & downright inconsiderate. After all, she's come all this way dragging her tattered life behind like a half-starved puppy. Oh, I know, you've been on that train before & missed every stop until it was too late. I'll give you that. But, just imagine how good the wine will taste & maybe there's a new one fresh & intact in her fat purse that's meant for you, one that will take you back to Paris & the right cards will be there when you need them & a second chance is all anyone can ask before the broker closes shop, the door locks behind & there's no one left for a quick Alley-Oop.

Is That Too Much

Is that too much to ask? Is that even possible? & if so, who will answer or even hear? It's come to that. Pallbearers, bailiffs & frightened jurists are all that are left along the road to gawk & flaunt, flirt & flounder. In the meantime, tanks roll down St. George Avenue chipping away at decency & harmonizing with whoever will cast the first stones. You'd think there would be recourse. Not likely. No one is left to pry the briars loose, no one to light the lamps. Those who remember remind us of the gangs that roamed the back country, women hiding in stale attics, men too frozen in time to even take a stab at truth, all this & kids born insane. When the last plane shot down the runway loaded with gold & the men who did the harvest, a small voice could be heard in the belfry: Stop-Stop-Stop the bells & all will be well.

Restrained Lust

Restrained-Lust strokes her hand & breathes his heat against her neck. Theirs is a mysterious coupling: he, with a gambler's cunning grace & questionable judgment, she, with a dancer's love of rhythm, poise & wanton exhibition. They've chosen to ignore Speculation-Without-Promise who inserts herself in the lives of strangers without thought of consequence. In the last scene, Elvis whinnies his way though the Carolinas coming to rest in Biloxi where Carnival is in full swing, crap-tables are full & center stage set for Rodeo. Our lovers are playing their parts without concern for the croupier with his wicked stick or the director with his menacing hook. What was once enigmatic is simply a diversion. They know better than we the odds, the tunes & the flawless steps to take.

When The Gavel

When the gavel sounds, Heaven-Help-Us squirms in her seat. & when she's asked to describe the circumstances of the night before, she demurs to Justice-For-All who quickly takes the floor & tosses it back in the face of Who-The-Hell-Cares. How's that for an opening salvo, says Might-Is-Right, rummaging in his bag of tricks before the lights go out & the elephants exchange rings & razzmatazz? Who can tell anymore? & who's to be trusted in this can-can world of doublespeak & double-up & double-cross where mountains are still made from mole hills & Quiet-Now competes with Bearing Arms for the last vote on the last day – before the next die is cast & the last man standing wears the crown & the mockingbird on his stained shoulder? His banner reading: One Hell Of A Ride – 25 cents.

She Was The Apple

She was the apple of his eye until another wormed her way into his leggings where all delicious decisions are upended, inspected & corrupted. From that disguise appears the first robin of spring or what passes as a robin but is possibly a blue jay or magpie or even an ocelot — No matter. Let's begin here: They're on the deck of his fancy yacht, she with her unruly temper & he with his need to fabricate history. It's finally 2 p.m. & time for their daily massage. She'll go first, down the stairs into the inner sanctum, he'll follow at a strategic distance — never can be too careful, especially now, with that unexpected blizzard offshore & their romantic geography under investigation. Here's all you need know: At the end of their rope — At the end of their mutual distraction, At the end of the coming attractions, Before all hell breaks loose, pass the popcorn.

Somewhere

Somewhere between then & now the skin on the model's face changed from chocolate brown to pale white & down the escalator she went tripping on oxy, crank & black-beauties carrying that grudge she'd nurtured since Pop left home & Mom decided there wasn't enough room under her twisted roof for the two of them & so it's been, from one watering hole to the next without thought of making good or breaking bad & here it's another moth-eaten day without Thanksgiving or Christmas to roust a few good-cheers as each rendezvous turns to mashed potatoes blocking out the sun or is it the Doctor's blind-spot sucking all the air from the room? & So she writes, "Let me know when you've had enough . . . you motherfucker" & the reply is a longtime coming if at all & all the while her ship slips its moorings & monkeys & . . . memories & . . . moonscapes & . . .

It's A Subterranean

It's a subterranean Monday night here in Painesville & the One-Time-Once Quartet is rousting the neighborhood with their eat 'em up rickey-rocky & when into the mix trots James-Earl with his clever-cleaver & rolled up socks it's everyone for themselves & around the corner the locomotives warble & whine & the lights change from green to red & here's-one-for-you gets tangled up with I've-warned-your-ass-before & by the time anyone noticed it was 4 a.m. & even the cops had booked & Grandma Betty-Ann could finally shutdown her emporium of sweet meats & tasty titillations & as the hint-of-the-day-to-come muscled its way out of the river, all you'd hear (if you'd made it this far) might be the tender breathing of baby Marcella & the whispered, "I love it when you do that" from behind the screen –

under the quilt –

        between the sheets –

                just down the hall.

Some Photographs

Some photographs take us back before Artificial Intel, before Smashed Atoms, internal-combustion or steam-driven horse chasers. Romance lurks there & it don't take much to coax her out before she's an animated shill at Carnival wishing us well & slipping a fiver to who-can-do-no-wrong while Max & his crew diddle the twins & wrestle Mikie for his thimble & Doxy for her trumpet & before long it's Hi-Ho time & the circus is in town with gorillas & poisonous bats & sharpened teeth & someone's left the trunk unlatched & out jumps Pandora & her singular brew of fliers & runners & go-get-um & I-got-mine & from the railing the twins pepper-spray the lot chanting "Come an Get it / Whatever you want / However you want it" & Come on down to Mama's place where the Juk-Juk jumps & all you gotta do is Yip-Yip Hurray & Hydy-Hy & slim-slim Haroo . . .

You May Wonder

You may wonder how it's done. How the machine is altered so perfectly as to deny alteration. How obliteration of eighty years can be accomplished in one. Rivers take eons to form, as do mountains & most mitigation. Have we been cruelly misled? It doesn't take a big foot to squash a muffin or a big fist to knock down a potent idea of escape & promise whose time has arrived but for the birthing. Those aren't fake signatures on that parchment, son. They're the evidence of men pondering perfection — to build, not to decimate. See how the black pussy rubs herself against the leg of the arrogant commissar, how he reaches down & sticks his finger in her vagina, wiggling & waggling until she capitulates? So much for fair play & a jolly good time was had, doncha know?

Especially Present

Especially present in the morning, she hovers above his bed like a will-o'-the-wisp & turns him loose to sail into the bleak & sterile, reaching deep for consolation in his bag of old tricks. He thought he'd buried his naiveté with his scripts, highlighting the dangers of unlocking that door. It seemed to work . . . then. Maybe he got, you know, razzle-dazzled. No. He's never been one to come too close. Until Linda. How he wobbled around in a daze without her & . . . Now he claims, better a fast car on a fast road, Macallans 25 @ 5 p.m. & a sweet woman with an inventive mouth to rev his engine & send him clowning up one side & down the other . . . There may be a better way. But, hey, who's to say?

She's Become

She'd become his obsession. An illusion? No. In the flesh. Mind & body. Fragile & illusive. It takes more than blood to run the motor. Take two at bedtime or wait in the dark for the intruder who will surely come. They'd been happy? No. Not exactly. A cautionary tale. At best. In for a penny in for a pound. How those old sayings distil. Don't lose touch. We're running out of time. Don't settle for alternatives. If she wants you back. If the frigate bird finds land. If the whale's breach means business. If. There are other options. Remember your promise. Remember to call at first light. Wear your heart like a trophy. Maybe there's a parley to be played. Not one to mess with fate. Or a fatalist. In the matter at hand, black is a hedge. Even obsessions get old & cold & even beg for relief. Here. Take my hand. No time left for supplication. Eat what's been prepared.

They Let Him

They let him out on the night of the full moon when the streets were jammed with everybody-for-themselves & tits-&-ass & johnny-be-good & out of the blue the saucer-patrol with every conceivable crusty & crank & ratchet & whistle & before you can say jimmy-crack-corn there's a stampede of Bison & fire in the gorge & war-weary families asleep in the gullies & team by team the riders assemble & win-one-for-everyman rings the gong & along comes Martha & we've-never-met & they join the chorus & sing the great goody-goody the uniquely-unread voted for & fuck-you-all voted for & who-gives-a-shit voted for & it's great to be alive & guzzling the Kool-Aid & laughing all the way to tomorrow even if tonight blows a tire & the end is much like the beginning & we'll-never-know wins the stuffed baboon, turns out the lights & double-locks the golden gate.

After Broken Teeth

After broken teeth & miles of spinning like a child's top. After mowing down trepidation. After gorging on bitter butter, alcohol & cocaine. After suicide & sleepwalking. After gaining ground. After losing temperament & a stutter-step. After bearing witness. After rejection. After a turn to the left. After granddaughters & macaroni. After more alcohol. After lying naked in the snow. After taking aim. After running the rapids, missing the mark & eating crow. After miscellaneous junkets & jackoffs. After burying the hatchet. After harvesting the potatoes of summer. After apple pie & frozen lakes. After sinister weather & skunks at play. After Marjorie & the minster's son. After the birthday party. After she threw you out. After much unsaid & much to learn. After lollipops & guillotines. After noon & abracadabra.

On His 60th Birthday

On his 60th birthday he smoked a cigar & drank a toast to his ancestors who he rarely thought of but this day they took a place in his living-room & in his bedroom with the thick black drapes & pictures of naked men & women & they drifted onto his porch where he sat smoking & drinking his afternoon wine & it's then he thought of her & the lashing he took when she cut him loose & how he'd been so vulnerable & in fact it was his birthday & he should be thrilled to be alive & he was but there was that damned vision of her naked & so nonchalant & it was then his great-grandfather stepped into the frame & blocked his view & asked for a cigar & raised a glass to begin a toast & it was then he admitted there was more to his life & more to its living than what might have been but would no longer be.

Big-Mouth

Big-Mouth tells us this time is no different than it was before or before that & after it's over it will be the same & he-who-really-reads warns us away from the stale-piece they've set before us & trouble-enough adjusts the volume on the machine & cranks it back to avoid the bright light that always follows the lies & body counts. She-who-can't-be-stopped motions for us to follow. Inside is as dark as outside & the-mewing-&-the-snarling insists we keep moving & we do to the end of the hall where old-eyes the clown turns bats into rabbits & rabbits into chattering monkeys who crawl the walls & whisper, "take back your dignity" & "you don't have to go along" & other such advice that's long overdue & he-of-another-mind offers to mediate & after the last person has had their say, the curtain is pulled back & out steps he-who-never-should–have-been with his riding crop & hand grenade & . . .

It's Colder Now

It's colder now. The man with a hook for a hand says so. Remember those who've passed by, he says. Wave 'Hi' to Timmy, the grocer's son & Evelyn, the Doctor's daughter & Harold, don't forget Harold, who cooked for grandma & Tom, the priest, who laid her to rest. & - Be sure to stop by Emma's for that afternoon delight she'd always promised & Willie's for the hundred he owes from that botched scam – you remember, the one where you put up the cash & he was suppose to but didn't. Something about leaving that always troubles the mind: Fear of failure? Fear of the randomness of travel? That recurring dread of being lost – without roots to keep you straight, to nourish new growth? Wait. There's the old guy with the hook again. Ask him. He's bound to have an answer that can ease the way. Never pass up the opportunity for salvation, even if it's temporary.

& So It Begins

& So It Begins

with a smile on a crowded metro when you're on your way to see the lady down the hall who is home with the flu & needs a prescription from the pharmacy & a bottle of bourbon for hot toddies & eggs for breakfast & who can tell what-else she has in mind this being April & the first signs of green already obvious in the dark loam outside the basement door.

*

with a memory of a walk in the woods behind the family home in Michigan with B & the deer that startled them on the path & violets & Monarch Butterflies & the gauzy texture of her underpants as you slid them from her open body on the bed of moss just off the trail behind the fallen oak on the cliff above the lake.

*

with the notes from D's piano slipping secretly from the safety of her studio to everyone's pleasure & the first sip of Sam Adams Lager on that hot day in New Mexico where the future was still a mystery to be entered into & the present all you would ever know of timelessness – a day when there is no past & only the prospect of becoming.

*

with a hoarse shout in the night from a passing car & a series of gunshots & police sirens & boots on stone & the cries of a fearful kid or one in pain & more cars & men's voices & red lights flashing & an ambulance & the cries of a fearful kid or one in pain or . . . ,

*

with the memory of the house where your father last lived before he died alone in a hospital bed drugged & finally free – but not you – you're still there at the other end of the country, hanging on the dismal words his doctor spoke, knocking back your third Johnny Walker Black, while your mind filled with those flimsy scenes – those flashcards of history – while that hot & bitter taste rose at the back of your throat & . . .

*

in the heat of a July afternoon on a bare mattress in the attic of an abandoned house in Jefferson, Missouri & fingers gently finding & feeling & probing the sensitive orifices of first her then him & as the play continues, there are fluids & muted sounds & lips seeking lips & lips seeking those same orifices & tongues & sweat & breath as thick as fog & the soggy, soggy heat . . .

*

with his daughter's drawing of a house framed against a thin blue sky with a red dot in the upper right corner where her brother Jose lives with his brothers & sisters who were sold to the men who put them in the care of Olivia & her dogs that pace back & forth in front of the cage where the three of them slept before they were taken away as was their mother & aunt before them & it was & it is & it will be as it has become . . .

*

with you all somber & slow strolling absently along the riverbank stopping here & there to look for frogs or turtles or a basking trout & trying to remember the last time she came to you & reached out her hand to touch your cheek, the last time she appeared anywhere close-by, close enough for you to reach out your hand & touch her cheek . . . these memories come slowly like a dazed dog maybe or a crippled heart pumping just enough blood . . .

*

step by step & hand over hand, sluggish as a tortoise, he eases into his assigned space, each one smaller than the last until there is nowhere to go, no one to reach down &, as if by magic, draw him up. It's then his father appears in the distance waving a newspaper with the headline **WAR DECLARED** & the rumble of tanks on cobblestones & there's Maria just out of reach & his calico cat, Tomas, & the ever steady & eternal rain.

*

 one lie after the other as the TV mocks & strains to discover a formal war-torn moment giving way instead to frame after frame of blood-soaked remorse. No. What we have here is the last of the fallen caught in a swirl of crisping skin & dust as the buzzards hover in expectation – not much here for these dark scavengers – not much left to celebrate or mourn . . . only the wind – only the bloody wind & a husky cough echoing from stage left . . . or was it stage right?

*

 with the river rising – Sandbags & prayers & loaded trucks, the family bible & Sonny's computer from school, Henry's *Maker's Mark* from Christmas & Aunt Holly's old rabbit coat, the last photo of Frank from Iraq & Buddy's purple heart, Stan's trophy from his last trip home & Beauty set free & . . . & mom cradles Beth in her lap & Gran in the driver's seat & the road ahead & the moon behind & the house & the barn & the river . . .

*

& So It Ends

on the cusp of a dream

      where an old battered Grizzly paws the sky

           roars once in rut or rage & vanishes,

                scarred coat & bloody teeth,

                      into the quivering air

About the Author

Born in Chicago, Roger Aplon was a founder and managing editor of Chicago's "CHOICE – A Magazine of Poetry & Photography" with John Logan & Aaron Siskind. He has had thirteen books published: one of prose poems & short fiction: _Intimacies_ & twelve of poetry, including the recently published: _Mustering What's Left – Selected & New Poems – 1976 – 2017_ from Unsolicited Press. Given his love of jazz & experimental music, he often reads his work with musicians from the Avant-Garde ensembles Wormhole (In Yokohama & Tokyo Japan) & the Trummerflora Collective (San Diego, CA). In the course of his long career he's been awarded many prizes and honors including an Arts Fellowship from the Helene Wurlitzer Foundation in Taos, New Mexico. After an eight year writing retreat in Barcelona Spain, he now makes his home in Beacon, New York where he edits & publishes a poetry magazine: "Waymark – Voices of the Valley. You can read and hear examples of his work at: www.rogeraplon.com

Other Books By Roger Aplon

Stiletto
By Dawn's Early Light At 120 Miles Per Hour
It's Mothers' Day
Barcelona Diary
The Man With His Back To The Room
Intimacies
It's Only TV
Improvisations: Poetic Impressions From Contemporary Music
Mustering What's Left – Selected & New Poems 1976 – 2017

Chapbooks

Improvisations I
After Goya
Escapades
Homage To A Widow

www.ingramcontent.com/pod-product-compliance
Lightning Source LLC
Chambersburg PA
CBHW051806100526
44592CB00016B/2586